For Lucy,
you know what you did.
—ANNABETH & CONNOR

To my wife, Liz—proof of
intelligent life on Earth.
—L.K.

Henry Holt and Company, *Publishers since 1866*

Henry Holt is a registered trademark of Macmillan Publishing Group, LLC

120 Broadway, New York, NY 10271 • mackids.com

Our books may be purchased in bulk for promotional, educational, or business use.

Please contact your local bookseller or the Macmillan Corporate and Premium Sales Department at

(800) 221-7945 ext. 5442 or by email at MacmillanSpecialMarkets@macmillan.com.

Library of Congress Control Number: 2023940733

First edition, 2024

Book design by Mike Burroughs

The illustrations in this book were created in Procreate.

Printed in China by RR Donnelley Asia Printing Solutions Ltd., Dongguan City, Guangdong Province

ISBN 978-1-250-22288-6

1 3 5 7 9 10 8 6 4 2

SPACE:

THE FINAL POOPING FRONTIER

Written by

Annabeth Bondor-Stone
and **Connor White**

Illustrated by

Lars Kenseth

GODWINBOOKS

Henry Holt and Company
New York

Everybody poops. So what's an astronaut to do when hurtling through space with zero gravity and zero privacy?

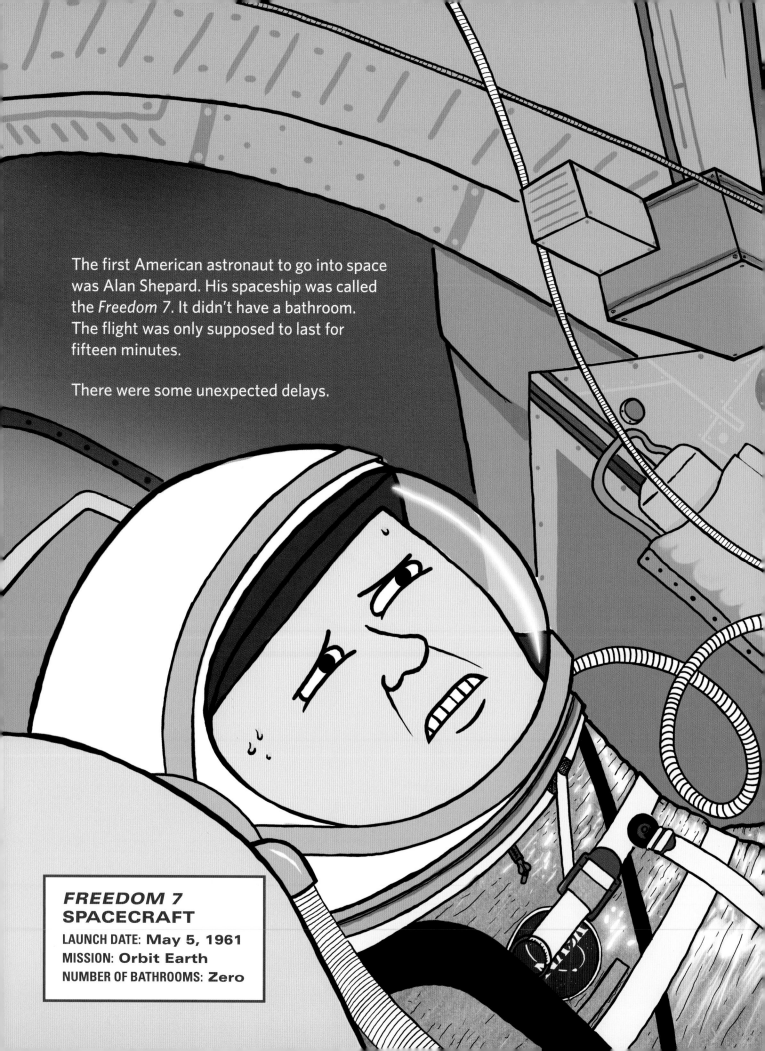

The first American astronaut to go into space was Alan Shepard. His spaceship was called the *Freedom 7*. It didn't have a bathroom. The flight was only supposed to last for fifteen minutes.

There were some unexpected delays.

FREEDOM 7
SPACECRAFT
LAUNCH DATE: May 5, 1961
MISSION: Orbit Earth
NUMBER OF BATHROOMS: Zero

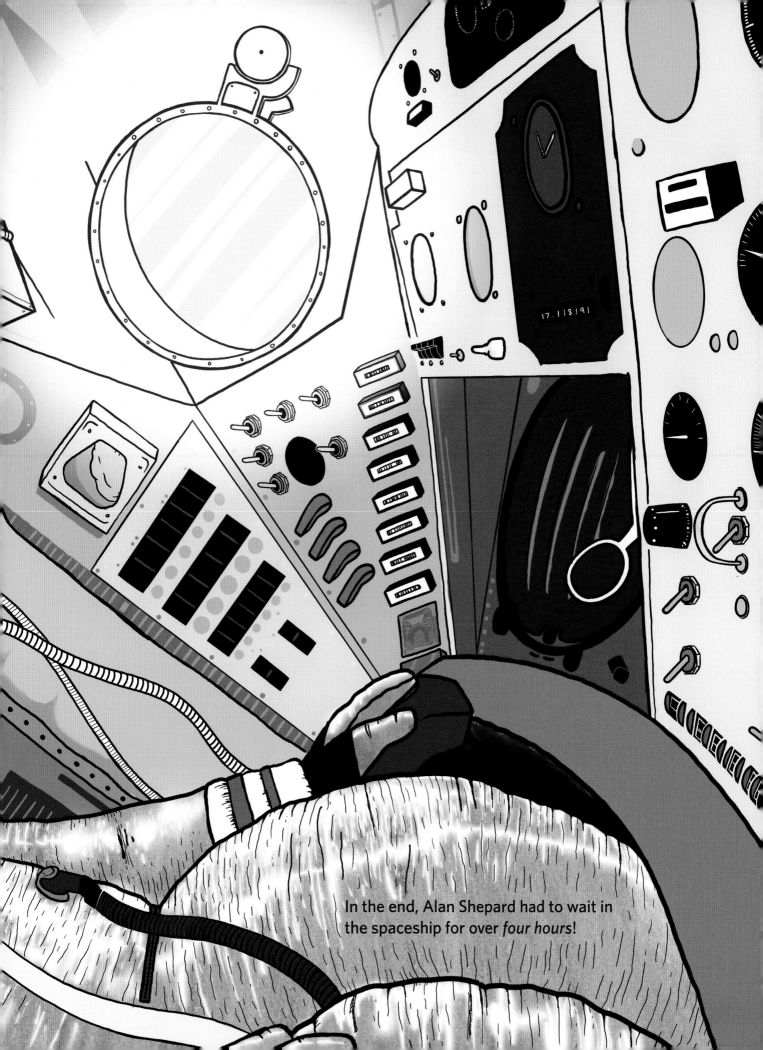

In the end, Alan Shepard had to wait in the spaceship for over *four hours*!

How were astronauts supposed to discover all the wonders of outer space and unravel the mysteries of the entire galaxy if they couldn't even *poop*?

The scientists at NASA had to find a solution to this problem. They had to keep the astronauts safe and healthy when they were thousands of miles from home—or even farther! After all, they had big dreams for the future of space travel.

National Aeronautics and Space Administration (NASA)
AGENCY IN CHARGE OF SPACE TRAVEL AND SPACE RESEARCH IN THE UNITED STATES

If astronauts were ever going to make it to these far-off places, they would have to spend a lot of time in space. They would have to be able to do normal things like eat, sleep, exercise, and, of course . . . poop!

Why not just put a toilet on a spaceship?

Gravity is different in outer space. What goes *down* on Earth might go *up*. So, things would get really messy.

Gravity wasn't the only challenge.
On Earth, toilets are connected to pipes.
But there's no plumbing in space.

Plus, early spaceships were very
cramped. Every ounce of extra weight
was expensive. There was no place to fit
a bathroom.

In the 1960s, NASA launched the Apollo space program. The goal was to send astronauts to the moon. The moon is 238,855 miles from Earth. Astronauts could expect to spend over a week in their spaceships.

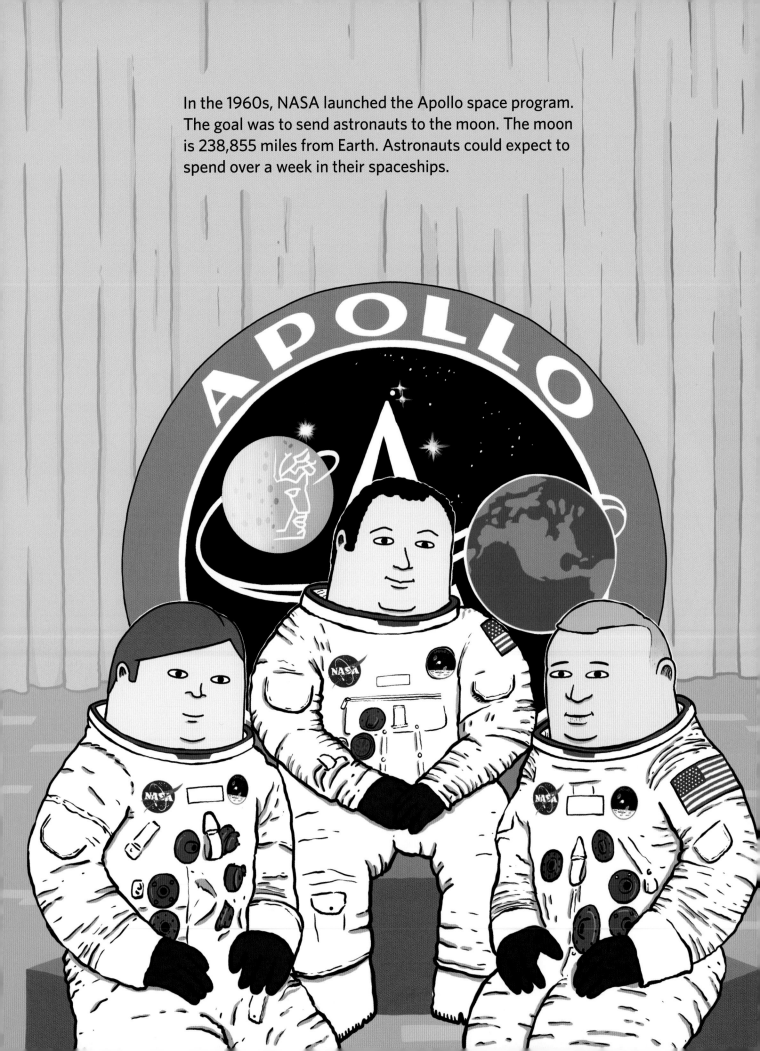

APOLLO SPACE PROGRAM
LAUNCH DATES: **October 11, 1968–December 7, 1972**
MISSION: **Land on the moon**
NUMBER OF BATHROOMS: **Still zero!**

So what did Apollo astronauts do?

When astronauts traveled to the moon, they brought clear plastic bags to poop in.

THE BAG WAS 1 FOOT LONG, WITH A 1.5-INCH OPENING AND A STICKY PART TO ATTACH TO THE ASTRONAUT'S BUTTOCKS.

When they were finished taking care of business, astronauts had to massage a chemical into their own poop to kill the bacteria.

Otherwise, the gases produced by the poop would expand . . . and explode the bag!

Since there was no separate bathroom area, there was no privacy. The astronauts had to go in the cockpit, which was about the size of the front seat of a small car.

VACANT

An excerpt of a conversation from the Apollo 10 mission:

LUNAR MODULAR PILOT EUGENE CERNAN:
"Where did that come from?"

COMMANDER THOMAS STAFFORD:
"Give me a napkin quick. There's a turd floating through the air."

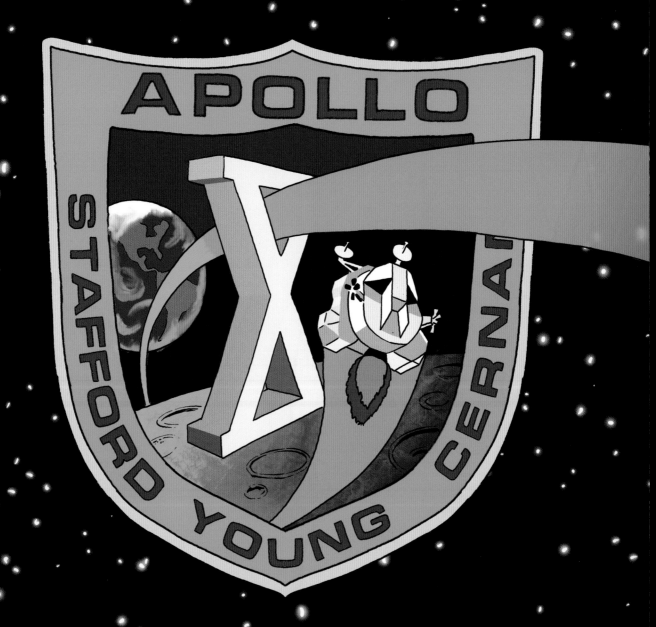

COMMAND MODULE PILOT JOHN YOUNG:
"I didn't do it. It ain't one of mine."

LMP CERNAN:
"I don't think it's one of mine."

CDR STAFFORD:
"Mine was a little more sticky than that. Throw that away."

CMP YOUNG:
"God almighty."

ALL THREE: (Laughter)

The Apollo space program was an enormous success.
On July 20, 1969, Neil Armstrong and Buzz Aldrin
became the first people to ever walk on the moon.

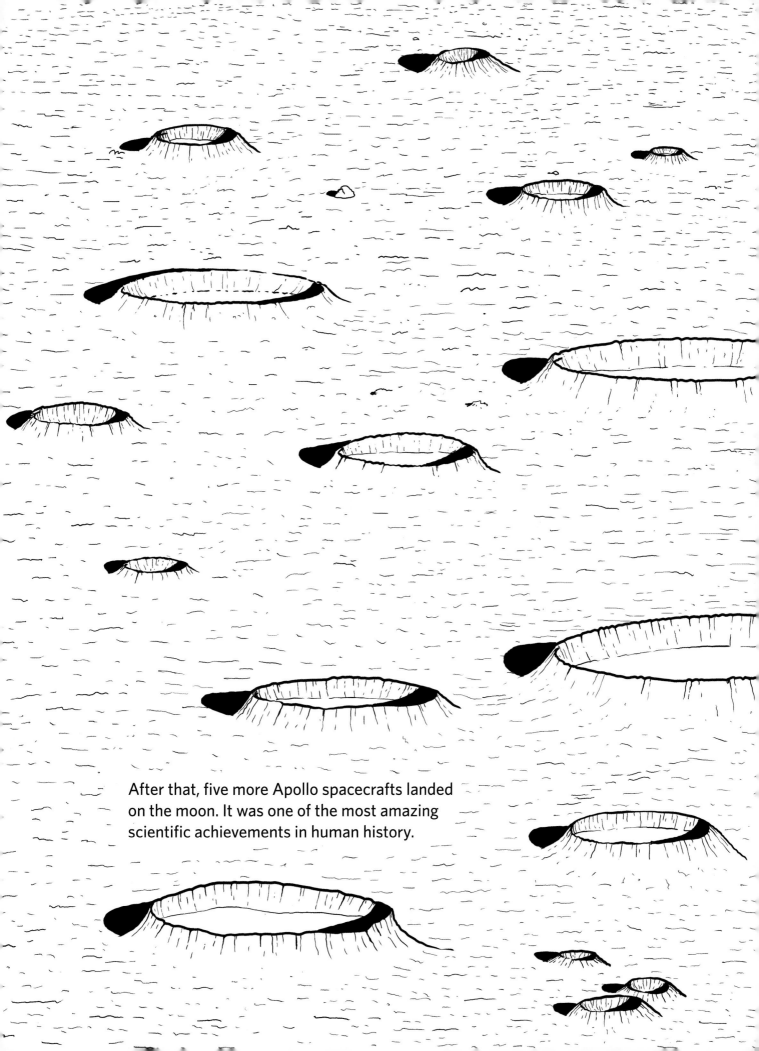

After that, five more Apollo spacecrafts landed on the moon. It was one of the most amazing scientific achievements in human history.

However, the astronauts still had one big complaint.

THIGH BARS
(TO KEEP ASTRONAUTS FROM FLOATING AWAY)

VERY SMALL OPENING

LEVER

FUNNEL

VACUUM CONTROLS
(TO SUCK POOP DOWN INTO THE TOILET)

FOOT RESTRAINTS

Back at NASA, scientists got to work inventing a toilet that could function in outer space.

RESTROOM

The space toilet was so different
from a regular toilet that astronauts
had to learn how to use it before
going into space.

There was a practice toilet at NASA headquarters.

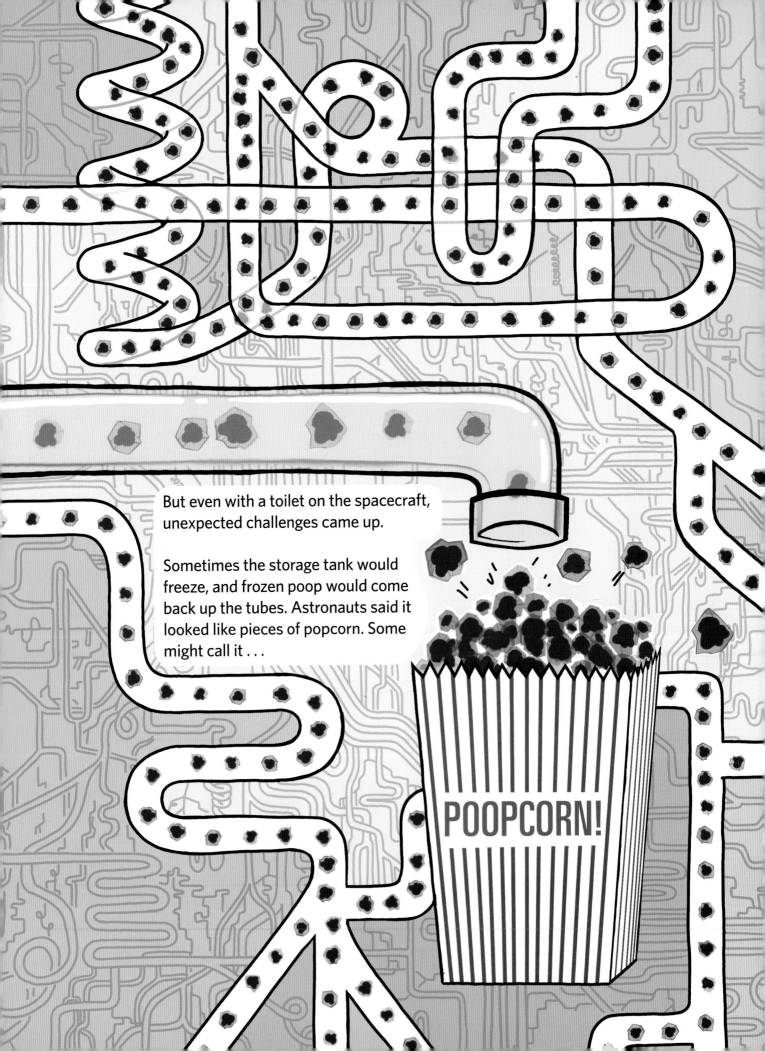

Even when everything was working perfectly, the process of going to the bathroom could take up to forty-five minutes.

Astronauts had to strip naked, close a curtain around the titanium toilet, and seal their butts to a 4-inch opening.

The invention of the space toilet made astronauts' lives much better, especially as more and more people visited outer space.

In 1998, a science lab called the International Space Station (ISS) was launched into space.

INTERNATIONAL SPACE STATION

LAUNCH DATE: November 20, 1998
MISSION: Scientific research
NUMBER OF BATHROOMS: Two!

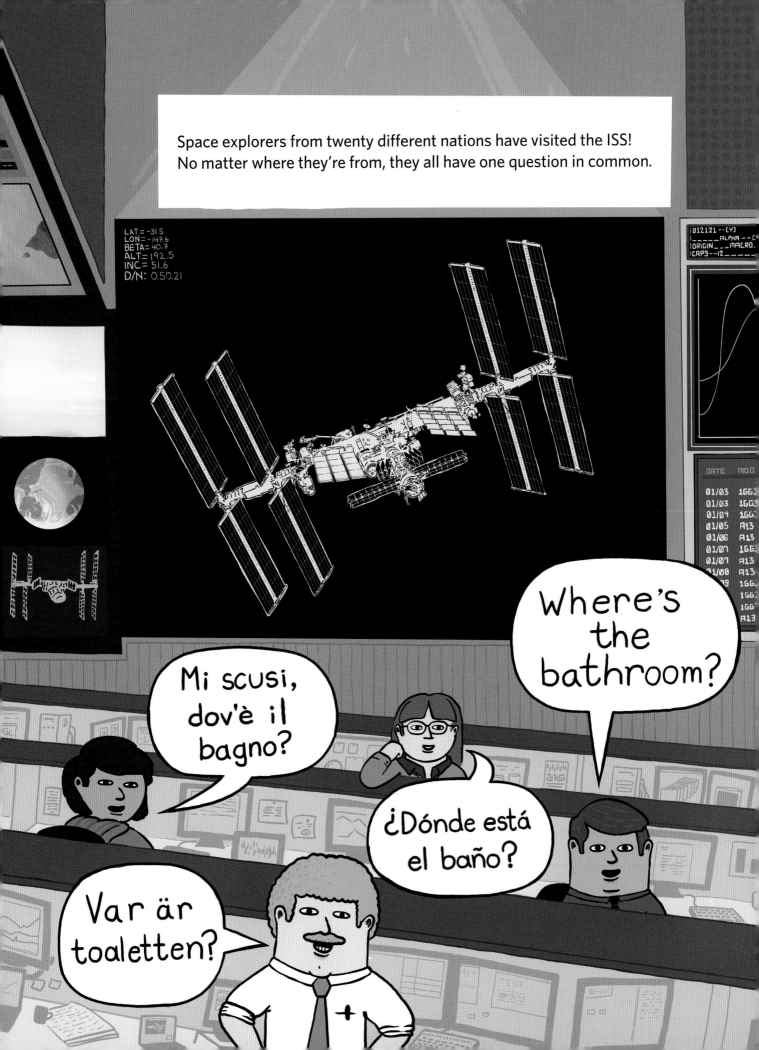

The ISS continues to orbit Earth today. Missions there often last for many months.

Astronauts named Mark Vande Hei (USA) and Pyotr Dubrov (RUS) spent 354 days, 14 hours, and 56 minutes there.

The more time people can comfortably spend on the ISS, the more cool stuff they can do. They even shot a music video there!

But astronauts don't want to have to rely on the space toilet.

What if they want to explore Mars for days at a time?

NASA wanted to make it possible for astronauts to be away from the space toilet for up to six days.

The only option they had was a diaper.

So in 2016, NASA launched the Space Poop Challenge.

People from all over the world put on their thinking caps so they could invent a better way to poop in space.

Twenty thousand competitors from one hundred and thirty countries submitted five thousand different ideas.

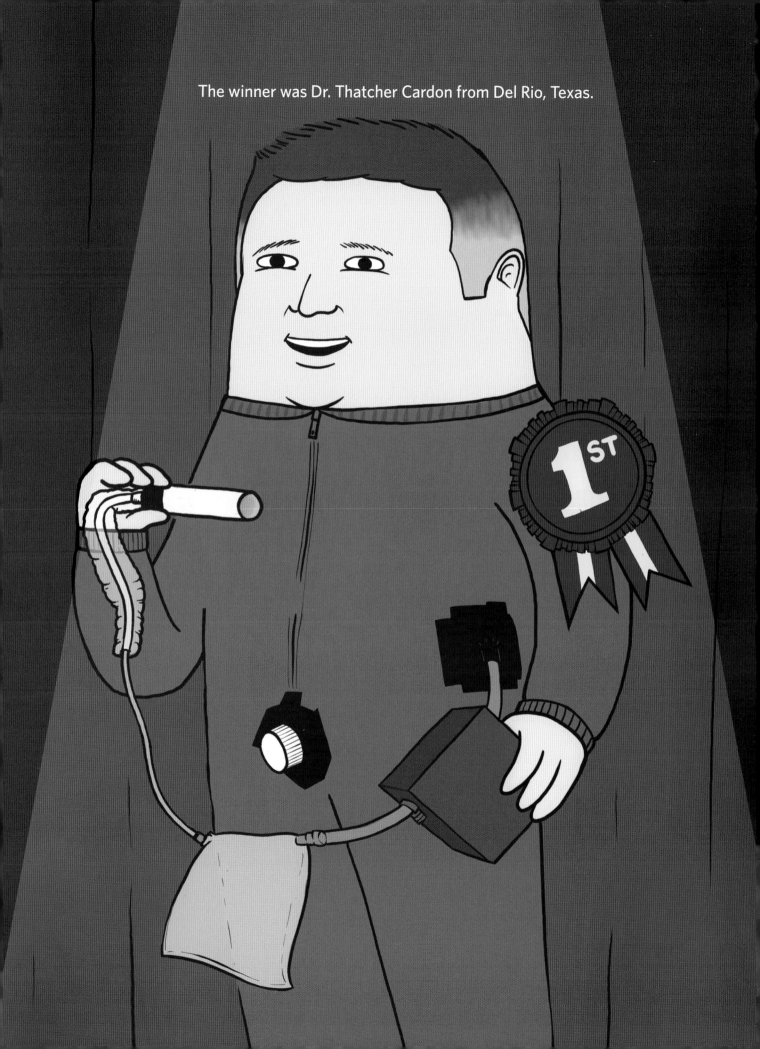

The winner was Dr. Thatcher Cardon from Del Rio, Texas.

Now, wherever astronauts go—they can *go*!

MORE POOP FUN FACTS
(AND BEYOND!)

THINK TWICE THE NEXT TIME YOU SEE A SHOOTING STAR.

Since astronauts don't have the luxury of flushing the toilet, they have to pack their poop into vacuum-sealed bags that get shot toward Earth. Due to the speed at which they're launched into space and the distance that they travel, these poop bags are effectively incinerated before ever reaching our planet. The next time you wish on a shooting star, remember, it might be a cargo ship full of poop burning up across the night sky!

THERE WAS A CAPITAL "PEE" PROBLEM ON THE FIRST AMERICAN SPACE EXPEDITION.

You may remember when we told you about Alan Shepard earlier; he was the astronaut who piloted America's first ever space expedition (which was supposed to last fifteen minutes but was significantly delayed for over four hours). What we didn't mention before was that Mr. Shepard, unfortunately, was not able to wait until the flight was completed to relieve his bladder—hopefully it's not too expensive to dry-clean a space suit!

REDUCE, REUSE, RECYCLE EVERYTHING. YES, EVERYTHING.

While astronaut poop is launched toward Earth, astronaut urine faces a very different fate. More often than not, while out in space, urine and sweat go through a purification process to become safe drinking water. This ingenious system helps eliminate the need for frequent resupply missions, allowing astronauts to spend longer stretches of time in space. Talk about un-*pee*-lievable!

WHAT'S NEXT?

Scientists are always working to improve conditions for astronauts, whether related to their experience on the toilet or otherwise. Researchers have already innovated ways to use poop and pee to grow edible bacteria for astronauts to eat on long-term missions; this is one of several poop-centered research efforts currently ongoing in the space-exploration community. Our poop contains minerals that may be too invaluable to flush away, or launch into space, on long-term space expeditions where resources are limited. As scientists work hard to improve space travel, it seems poop will continue to be an important part of the equation.

The future and feces go hand in hand!

SOURCES

Brueck, Hilary. "A NASA Astronaut Who Spent 665 Days Circling the Planet Reveals the Misery of Going to the Bathroom in Space." *Business Insider*, 26 May 2018, www.businessinsider.com/how-you-go-to-bathroom-space-nasa-astronaut-2018-5.

Dunbar, Brian. "Waste Not." *NASA*, 4 June 2004, www.nasa.gov/vision/earth/technologies/18may_wastenot.html.

"Boldly Go! NASA's New Space Toilet Offers More Comfort, Improved Efficiency for Deep Space Missions." *NASA*, 17 Sept. 2020, www.nasa.gov/feature/boldly-go-nasa-s-new-space-toilet-offers-more-comfort-improved-efficiency-for-deep-space/.

Gregg, Tracy. "How Do Astronauts Go to the Bathroom in Space?" *University at Buffalo College of Arts and Sciences*, 26 Jan. 2022, arts-sciences.buffalo.edu/news-and-events/recent-news/2021/march/gregg conversation-bathroom-space.html.

Hurt, Avery. "How Astronauts Go to the Bathroom in Outer Space." *Discover*, 1 Sept. 2021, www.discovermagazine.com/the-sciences/how-astronauts-go-to-the-bathroom-in-outer-space.

Kekatos, Mary. "NASA Says 98% of Astronauts' Urine, Sweat Can Be Recycled into Drinking Water." *ABC News*, 27 June 2023, abcnews.go.com/US/nasa-98-astronauts-urine-sweat-recycled-drinking-water/story?id=100406385.

Nelson, Bryn. "How Recycled Astronaut Poop Might Sustain a Mission to Mars." *NBC News*, 12 Feb. 2018, www.nbcnews.com/mach/science/how-recycled-astronaut-poop-might-sustain-mission-mars-ncna846281.

Reiss, Raytchle. "How Do Astronauts Go to the Bathroom in Space?" *Space Facts*, 1 Jan. 2023, www.space-facts.co.uk/how-do-astronauts-go-to-the-bathroom-in-space.

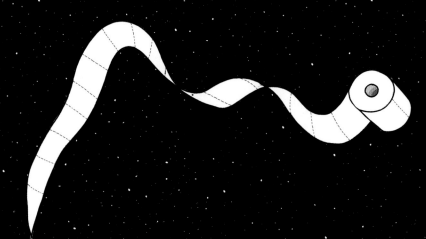